Great Source

Reading Advantage

Student Journal

Laura Robb • James F. Baumann • Carol J. Fuhler • Joan Kindig

Avon Cowell • Craig Roney • Jo Worthy

GREaT SOURCe®
EDUCATION GROUP
A Division of Houghton Mifflin Company

Contents

Cities **Magazine**

Name _____ Date _____

Building Vocabulary: Making Associations

Pick two words from the vocabulary list below. Think about what you already know about each word. Then answer the following questions.

claim	sightings	sonar
loch	plaster casts	

Word _____

What do you think about when you read this word? _____

_____

Who might use this word? _____

_____

What do you already know about this word? _____

_____

Word _____

What do you think about when you read this word? _____

_____

Who might use this word? _____

_____

What do you already know about this word? _____

_____

Now watch for these words in the magazine selection. Were you on the right track?

Writing: K-W-L Chart

Write two or three short sentences in the first column to tell what you know or think you know about the Loch Ness monster. Then write two or three questions in the second column that you would like answered about the Loch Ness monster. After reading the selection, fill in the last column.

Title _____

K What I Know	W What I Want to Know	L What I Learned

Name _____ Date _____

Building Vocabulary: Words with Multiple Meanings

Write two definitions for each word below.

Word	First Definition	Second Definition
cast	a plaster form	a group of people who perform in a play
bus		
spotted		
leaves		
view		
drove		

Building Vocabulary: Predictions

How do you predict these words will be used in "What Happened to Amelia Earhart?" Write your answers in the second column. Next, read the article. Then clarify your answers in the third column.

Word	My prediction for how the word will be used	How the word was actually used
solo		
social worker		
justify		
equator		
navigator		

Name _____

Date _____

Writing: Time Line

Make a time line showing six of the most important events in Amelia
Earhart's life. The first important event has been given.

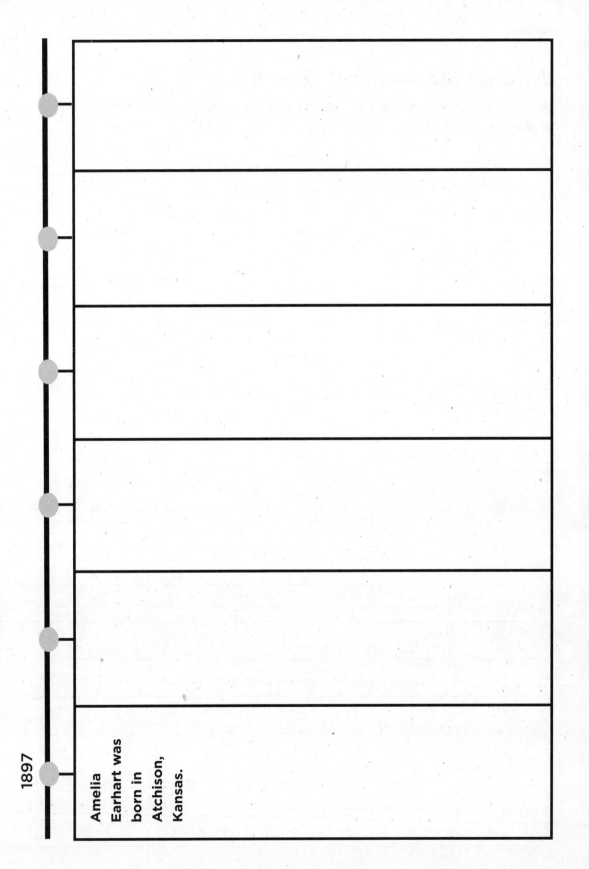

1897

Amelia
Earhart was
born in
Atchison,
Kansas.

Writing: Biographical Sketch

Use the time line on page 5 to write a short biographical sketch
of Amelia Earhart's life.

_____

_____

_____

_____

_____

_____

_____

_____

_____

_____

_____

_____

_____

_____

_____

_____

_____

Building Vocabulary: Combining Form *equi-*

Write examples and meanings of words with the combining form *equi* in the chart. One answer is given.

---
equi means "equal"

Examples	Meanings
1. equator	imaginary circle that divides Earth from top to bottom
2.	
3.	
4.	
5.	

Building Vocabulary: Making Associations

Pick two words from the vocabulary list below. Think about what you already know about each word. Then answer the following questions.

legends	carve
altars	chants

Word _____

What do you think about when you read this word? _____
_____

Who might use this word? _____
_____

What do you already know about this word? _____
_____

Word _____

What do you think about when you read this word? _____
_____

Who might use this word? _____
_____

What do you already know about this word? _____
_____

Now watch for these words in the magazine selection. Were you on the right track?

Name _____ Date _____

Writing: 5Ws and a Summary

The 5Ws—*who, what, where, when,* and *why*—give readers the basic information about what happens in an article or a section of an article. What do the 5Ws tell you about Mystery 8, the section that tells how the islanders made their statues? Complete the chart. Use the basic information in the chart to write a summary of how the islanders made their statues. Write your summary on another sheet of paper.

5Ws	Information from "Easter Island"
Who made the statues?	
What did they do to make the statues?	
Where did the major events take place?	
When did the major events take place?	
Why are the events important?	

Building Vocabulary: Homophones

Write homophone pairs you know. Then write a definition
for each word in the pair.

Homophones	Definitions
altar	a raised place where religious services are performed
alter	to change

Building Vocabulary: Knowledge Rating Chart

Show your knowledge of each word by adding information to the
other boxes in the row.

Word	Define or Use in a Sentence	Where Have I Seen or Heard It?	How Is It Used in the Selection?	Looks Like (Words or Sketch)
migrate				
breeding grounds				
generations				
nectar				
echolocating				
funnels				
environment				

Writing: Notes for Visualizing

Which part of the article could you visualize best? Describe that part below. Then draw a picture to show what you "saw" in your mind.

The part I could visualize best was _____

_____

_____

Some details I "saw" in my mind include _____

_____

_____

_____

Now draw what you visualized.

Building Vocabulary: Compound Words

Write four compound words. Then write each word that is part
of each compound. Write a definition of the compound using the
combined meanings of the two words that are part of it.

Compound Word	Word 1	Word 2	Definition of Compound Word
echolocating	echo	locating	finding something using repeated sounds

Building Vocabulary: Predictions

How do you predict these words will be used in "Optical Illusions"?
Write your answers in the second column. Next, read the article.
Then, clarify your answers in the third column.

Word	My prediction for how the word will be used	How the word was actually used
optical illusions		
complicated		
foreground		

Writing: Using Details to Visualize

Look at optical illusion 5. What pictures did you see? What were some of the details?

What I saw first was _____

Some details I saw were _____

What I saw next was _____

Some details I saw were _____

Choose one of your visualizations to illustrate.

Building Vocabulary: Using Context to Understand a Word

Select one of the words—*complicated* or *illusion*—that you defined
from the context. Complete these statements and answer these
questions about the word.

My Word in Context:

I think this word means _____

_____

because _____

_____

My word is _____

My word is not _____

Where else might I find this word? _____

What makes this an important word to know? _____

_____

_____

_____

_____

Building Vocabulary: Synonym and Antonym Chart

Read each vocabulary word. Think of three other words that are synonyms (similar in meaning) for it. Then think of three words that are antonyms (opposites) for the word. Use a thesaurus to help you.

Vocabulary Word	Synonyms	Antonyms
theft	1. robbery 2. 3.	1. donation 2. 3.
outrageous	1. 2. 3.	1. 2. 3.
disgusted	1. 2. 3.	1. 2. 3.

Writing: Story String

Choose one of the mini mysteries you read. Record the most important events in the order in which they happened.

What Happens First

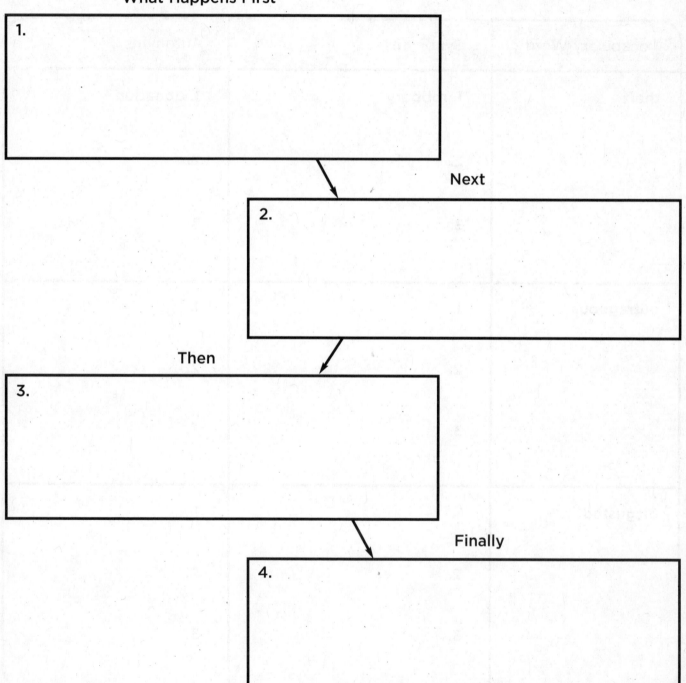

1.

Next

2.

Then

3.

Finally

4.

Name _____ Date _____

Writing: A Mini Mystery

What will happen first? What will happen next? How will the mystery
be solved? Who will the characters be? Write a mini mystery below.

_____

_____

_____

_____

_____

_____

_____

_____

_____

_____

_____

_____

_____

_____

_____

_____

_____

Building Vocabulary: Words with Multiple Meanings

Write two definitions for each word below.

Word	First Definition	Second Definition
framed	made to look guilty through false evidence	put into a border
hang		
trail		
race		
stand		

Building Vocabulary: Making Associations

Think about what you already know about the vocabulary words
alias and *elementary*. Then answer the following questions for
each word.

Word _____ **alias** _____

What do you think about when you read this word? _____
_____

Who might use this word? _____
_____

What do you already know about this word? _____
_____

Word _____ **elementary** _____

What do you think about when you read this word? _____
_____

Who might use this word? _____
_____

What do you already know about this word? _____
_____

Now watch for these words in the magazine selection. Were you on the right track?

Writing: Notes for Visualizing

Which part of the play could you visualize best? Describe that part
below. Then draw a picture to show what you "saw" in your mind.

The part I could visualize best was _____

_____

_____

Some details I "saw" in my mind include _____

_____

_____

_____

Now draw what you visualized.

Name _____ Date _____

Building Vocabulary: Words with Multiple Meanings

Write two definitions for each word below.

Word	First Definition	Second Definition
elementary	basic	a kind of school
place		
play		
pounds		

Building Vocabulary: Predictions

How do you think these words will be used in "Detectives at Work"?
Write your answers in the second column. Next, read the article.
Then, clarify your answers in the third column.

Word	My prediction for how the word will be used	How the word was actually used
forensic		
impressions		
foil		
splattered		
victim		
suspect		

Name _____ Date _____

Writing: A One-Minute Mystery

Visualize yourself as a detective. Read the questions detectives usually ask. With a partner, write answers that you can use to write a short mystery story together. Use a separate sheet of paper for the story and write the solution to your mystery on the back. Remember to title the story!

Detectives' Questions	Answers
Who is the mystery about?	
What happens in the mystery?	
Where does the mystery happen?	
When does the mystery happen?	
Why does the mystery happen?	
How does the mystery get solved?	

Building Vocabulary: Words with Multiple Meanings

Write two definitions for each word below.

Word	First Definition	Second Definition
foil	a thin metallic paper	to outwit or prevent
lying		
seal		
trace		

Building Vocabulary: Using a Word Map

Write a vocabulary word in the center box. Write a definition.
Next read the selection. Then answer the questions.

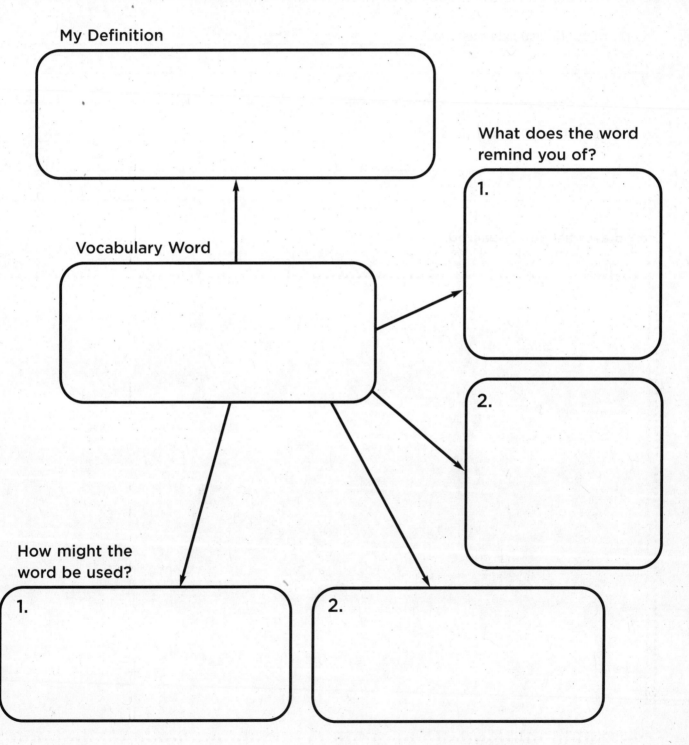

My Definition

Vocabulary Word

What does the word remind you of?

1.

2.

How might the word be used?

1.

2.

Comprehension: Notes for Visualizing

Which part of the article could you visualize best? Describe that part below. Then draw a picture to show what you "saw" in your mind.

The part I could visualize best was _____

_____

_____

Some details I "saw" in my mind include _____

_____

_____

Now draw what you visualized.

Building Vocabulary: Related Words

Pick a word you are familiar with as the key word. Then write three
or four words that are related to the key word. Write the part of
speech and the definition of each related word.

Related Words	Part of Speech	Definition
Key word: **mummy** 1. **mummify**	**verb**	**to make into a mummy by embalming**
2. **mummification**		
3.		
4.		
Key word: 1.		
2.		
3.		
4.		

Building Vocabulary: Making Associations

Think about what you already know about each vocabulary word.
Then answer the questions for each word.

Word _____ **charter** _____

What do you think about when you read this word? _____
_____

Who might use this word? _____
_____

What do you already know about this word? _____
_____

Word _____ **colony** _____

What do you think about when you read this word? _____
_____

Who might use this word? _____
_____

What do you already know about this word? _____
_____

Now watch for these words in the magazine selection. Were you on the right track?

Name _____ Date _____

Writing: Journal Entries

Write two journal entries as if you were one of the settlers on
Roanoke Island. Try to incorporate answers to these questions:
Where did the Roanoke settlers go? Why did they leave the island?

June 1, 1590	June 2, 1590

Building Vocabulary: Words with Multiple Meanings

Write two definitions for each word below.

Word	First Definition	Second Definition
charter	**a document given by a ruler, granting the right to do an activity**	**to hire**
coast		
ship		
back		

Building Vocabulary: Predictions

How do you predict these words will be used in "Code Talkers"?
Write your answers in the second column. Next, read the article.
Then, clarify your answers in the third column.

Word	My prediction for how the word will be used	How the word was actually used
under fire		
unbreakable		
Navajo		
ambush		

Writing: The 5Ws

The 5Ws—*who, what, where, when* and *why*—give readers the basic information about what happens in an article. What do the 5Ws tell you about "Code Talkers"? Fill in the chart below.

5Ws	Information from "Code Talkers"
Who or what is the article about?	
What happens in the article?	
Where does the major event of the article take place?	
When does the major event of the article take place?	
Why is this event important?	

Name .... Date ....

Writing: A Summary

Using the 5Ws chart from page 34, write a summary paragraph about how the Navajo Code was created.

_____

_____

_____

_____

_____

_____

_____

_____

_____

_____

_____

_____

_____

_____

Building Vocabulary: Using Context to Understand a Word

Complete the statements and answer the questions about the word
ambush.

My Word in Context:

I think this word means _____

_____

because _____

_____

_____

_____

My word is _____

_____

My word is not _____

_____

Where else might I find this word? _____

_____

What makes this an important word to know? _____

_____

_____

Name _____ Date _____

Building Vocabulary: Knowledge Rating Chart

Show your knowledge of each word by adding information to the other boxes in the row.

Word	Define or Use in a Sentence	Where Have I Seen or Heard It?	How Is It Used in the Selection?	Looks Like (Words or Sketch)
ruthless				
tomb				
archaeologists				
terra cotta				
chariots				
legend				

Writing: Notes for Visualizing

Which part of the article could you visualize best? Describe
that part below. Then draw a picture to show what you "saw"
in your mind.

The part I could visualize best was _____

_____

_____

Some details I "saw" in my mind include _____

_____

_____

_____

Now draw what you visualized.

Building Vocabulary: Word Root *terr*

Write words you know that contain the Latin root *terr*. Write a definition for each word. Use a dictionary to help you, if you wish.

Terr means "earth" or "land."

Words	Definitions
terra cotta	a reddish-brown clay

Building Vocabulary: Using a Word Map

Write a vocabulary word in the center box. Write a definition.
Next read the selection. Then answer the two questions.

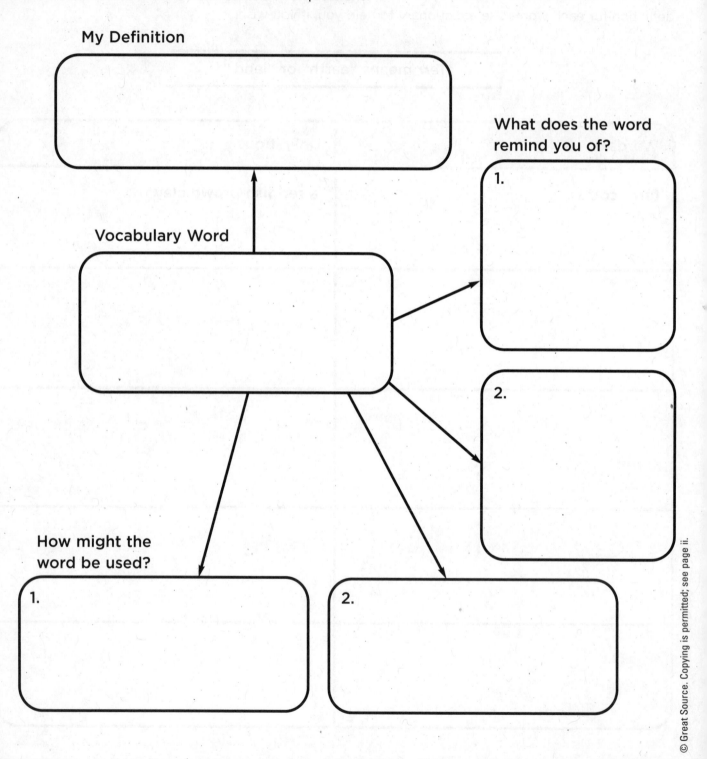

My Definition

Vocabulary Word

What does the word remind you of?

1.

2.

How might the word be used?

1.

2.

Writing: Double-Entry Journal

In the left-hand column, write five questions you think the selection might answer. Then read to see if your questions are answered. Write the answers in the right-hand column.

Questions I Hope to Answer	Answers to My Questions
1.	1.
2.	2.
3.	3.
4.	4.
5.	5.

Building Vocabulary: Acronyms

Work with a partner to find out what these acronyms stand for.
Consult a dictionary, if necessary. Then underline the letters used
to form the acronym.

Acronym	Abbreviation for
NASA	
RADAR	
LASER	
SCUBA	
ASAP	

Building Vocabulary: Predictions

How do you predict these words will be used in "Moon Walk"? Write
your answers in the second column. Then read the article. Clarify
your answers in the third column.

Word	My prediction for how the word will be used	How the word was actually used
vehicles		
lunar module		
gravity		
dock		
quarantine		

Writing: Illustrate and Label Spacecraft

Draw a picture of what you think the three vehicles that made the first trip to the moon looked like. Here are some labels and information to help you with your drawing.

Apollo 11	Name of the spacecraft that carried the other vehicles
Columbia	Name of the command module
Eagle	Name of the lunar module

Name _____   Date _____

Building Vocabulary: Word Web

Work with a partner to list as many words as you can that
contain the root *astro*. Check your words in a dictionary.

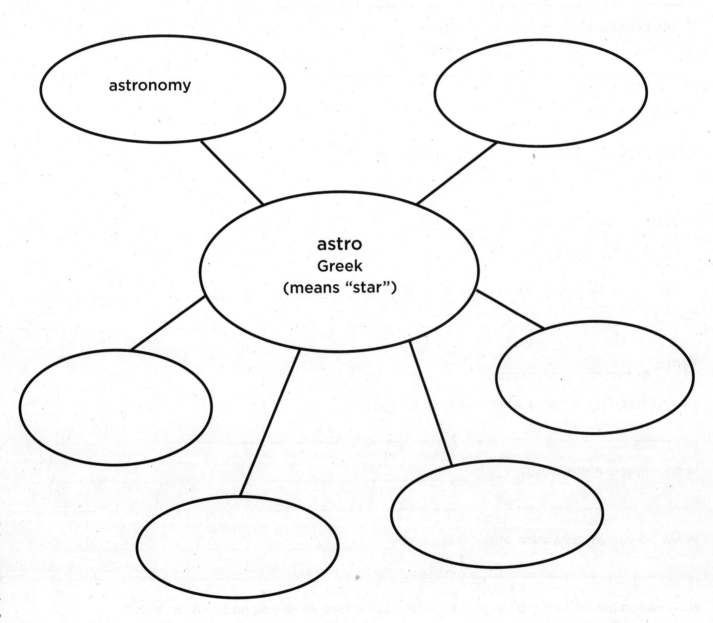

Building Vocabulary: Making Associations

Choose two vocabulary words. Think about what you already know about each word. Then answer the questions for each word.

air pressure	resist	misson
fabrics	ignite	

Word _____

What do you think about when you read this word? _____

_____

Who might use this word? _____

_____

What do you already know about this word? _____

_____

Word _____

What do you think about when you read this word? _____

_____

Who might use this word? _____

_____

What do you already know about this word? _____

_____

Now watch for these words in the magazine selection. Were you on the right track?

Writing: Labeled Illustration

Draw a sketch of an EMU (Extravehicular Mobility Unit). Label
the parts of the space suit. Refer to your drawing as you complete
the next page.

Writing: Explanatory Paragraph

List two special features of the EMU you might explain to a friend or family member. Jot down notes you would like to include in an explanation of these features.

Feature: _____ **Notes:** _____

_____

Feature: _____ **Notes:** _____

_____

Now use your notes to write an explanatory paragraph about the features you named.

_____

_____

_____

_____

_____

_____

_____

_____

_____

_____

_____

Building Vocabulary: Words with Multiple Meanings

Write two definitions for each word listed below.

Word	First Definition	Second Definition
vacuum	an appliance used for cleaning	emptiness of space
suit		
space		
patch		
mission		

Building Vocabulary: Knowledge Rating Chart

Show what you know about each word or phrase by completing the boxes.

Word	Define or Use in a Sentence	Where Have I Seen or Heard It?	How Is It Used in the Selection?	Looks Like (Words or Sketch)
customs				
engineering				
simulator				
weightless				
technology				
optical system				
monitors				
prevented				
video conference call				

Name _____ Date _____

Writing: A Friendly Letter

Write a letter to one of the astronauts. Tell about a dream
you have and what you are going to do to make that dream
come true.

_____

_____

_____

Dear _____,

_____

_____

_____

_____

_____

_____

_____

_____

_____

_____

_____

Building Vocabulary: Word Associations

Choose two words from the vocabulary list below. Think about what you already know about each word. Then answer the following questions.

engineering	simulator	weightless	technology
optical system	monitors	prevented	video conference call

Word _____

What do you think about when you read this word? _____
_____

Who might use this word? _____
_____

What do you already know about this word? _____
_____

Word _____

What do you think about when you read this word? _____
_____

Who might use this word? _____
_____

What do you already know about this word? _____
_____

Name _____   Date _____

Building Vocabulary: Creating a Word Web

Choose a vocabulary word for the center oval. Write the definition in the box at the bottom of the page. After you read the selection, add details around the oval that help to define the word.

habitats	deployed	weightlessness	momentum
briefing	commander	zero gravity	

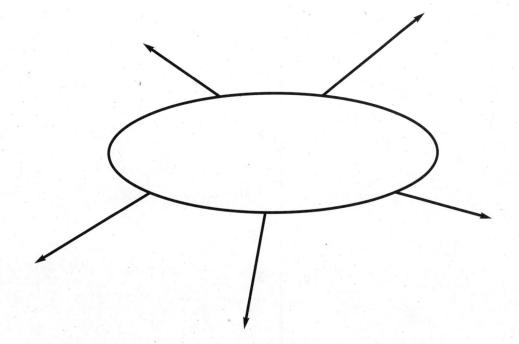

Write the complete definition here:

Writing: T-Chart

Compare and contrast the experiences that the campers have at Space Camp with the real experiences astronauts have in space.

Compare and Contrast

Campers at Space Camp	Real Astronauts
1. They sleep in habitats that look like the living areas on the ISS.	1. They sleep in living areas called habitats on the ISS.
2.	2.
3.	3.
4.	4.

Building Vocabulary: Suffixes *-er, -or*

The ending *-or* changes the verb *simulate* to a noun, *simulator*. Add or take away the suffix *-or* or *-er* to words you know to make verb and noun pairs. Write a definition for each word. Think of your own words for the last box.

Suffixes *-er, -or*

Words	Definitions
simulate	**imitate**
simulator	**a device that reproduces conditions**
act	
write	

Building Vocabulary: Predictions

How do you predict these words will be used in "Blaze"? Write your answers in the second column. Then read the story. Clarify your answers in the third column.

Word	My prediction for how the word will be used	How the word was actually used
harvest		
dome		
pioneer		
Martian		

Name _____ Date _____

Writing: Venn Diagram

Complete the Venn diagram to compare and contrast life on
Earth with life on Mars. Write the differences under the names
of the planets. Write the similarities under "Both."

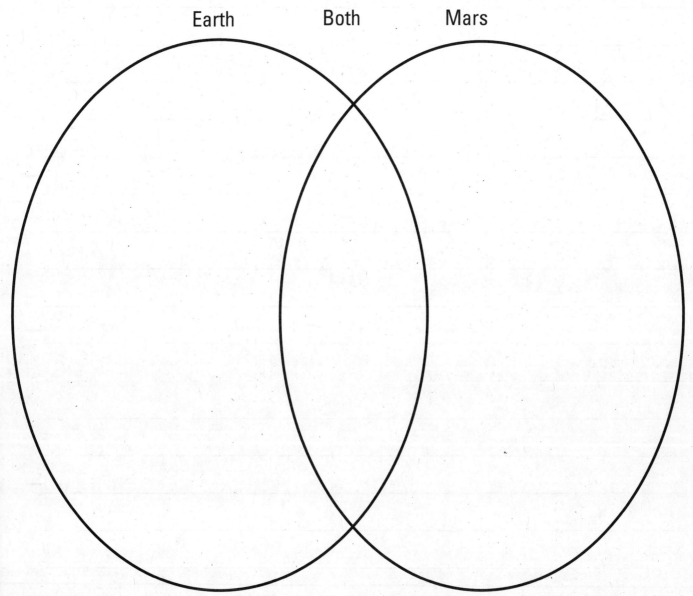

Earth   Both   Mars

Writing: Compare and Contrast

Use the information from your Venn diagram on page 57 to write a paragraph that compares and contrasts life on Earth with life on Mars.

_____

_____

_____

_____

_____

_____

_____

_____

_____

_____

_____

_____

_____

_____

_____

_____

_____

_____

Building Vocabulary: Noun Suffixes

Look at the suffixes that mean "one who." Use them to make up words to name beings from the different planets. Write sentences to describe your beings.

-an, -ian	Ohioan, Bostonian		*-ese*	Chinese
-ite, -tite	Akronite		*-ist*	tourist
-er, -ar, -or	Clevelander		*-ling*	duckling

Mars _____

_____

Venus _____

_____

Earth _____

_____

Mercury _____

_____

Jupiter _____

_____

Saturn _____

_____

Uranus _____

_____

Neptune _____

_____

Pluto _____

_____

Building Vocabulary: Knowledge Rating Chart

Show your knowledge of each word by adding information
to the other boxes in the row.

Word	Define or Use in a Sentence	Where Have I Seen or Heard It?	How Is It Used in the Selection?	Looks Like (Words or Sketch)
meteor				
shocking				
jammed				

Name .... Date ....

Writing: Somebody Wanted But So

Use this chart to help you organize your thoughts for a summary of "Visitors from Mars." After you fill in the chart, use your notes to write a paragraph that summarizes the play. You can write your paragraph on page 62.

	Notes
Somebody (main character)	
Wanted (key problem with details)	
But (conflict for the character)	
So (an outcome)	

Writing: Play Summary

Use your notes from the Somebody Wanted But So chart on
page 61 to write a summary of the play "Visitors from Mars."

_____

_____

_____

_____

_____

_____

_____

_____

_____

_____

_____

_____

_____

_____

_____

_____

_____

Building Vocabulary: Word Relationships

Complete the arrays for four other word pairs of your choosing.
Arrange your words so that they are ranked by graduated
degrees of relationship. Possible pairs to begin with include
hot/cold, *fast/slow*, and *quiet/noisy*.

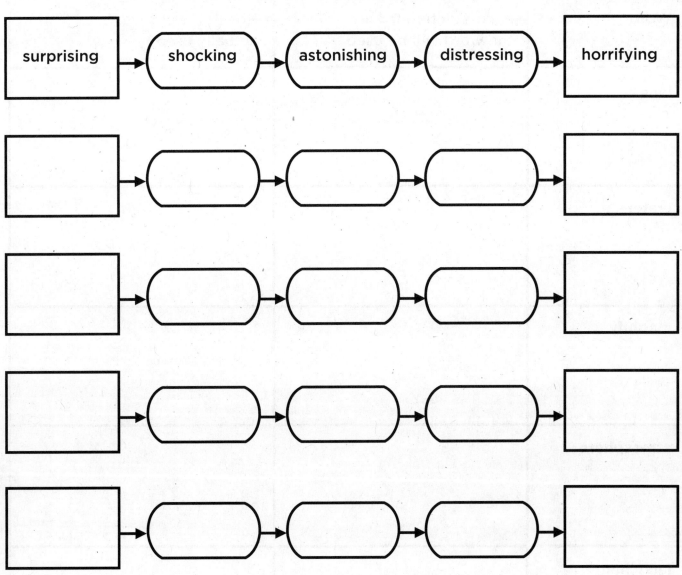

Building Vocabulary: Predictions

How do you predict these words will be used in "The Telescope"? Write your answers in the second column. Then read the article. Clarify your answers in the third column.

Word	My prediction for how the word will be used	How the word was actually used
lens		
craters		
magnify		
atmosphere		
launched		

Name _____ Date _____

Writing: Double-Entry Journal

Read each quotation from "The Telescope." Write what you
think it means. Refer to the article if you need more context.

Quotation	What You Think This Means
People who study history are not certain who really invented the telescope.	
As a scientist, he (Galileo Galilei) was a great star.	
People used to believe that the planets and stars moved around Earth.	
Telescopes have come a long way.	
He (Sir Isaac Newton) learned that white light is made up of all colors of light.	

Building Vocabulary: Word Part *tele*

Find six *tele* words in the puzzle by connecting letters that are next to each other. (You can move up, down, right, left, and diagonally. But you can't skip over letters!) Write the words you find on the lines below.

x	e	m	a	r
i	s	i	v	g
o	t	e	l	e
n	o	h	p	g
e	o	t	a	r

1. _____

2. _____

3. _____

4. _____

5. _____

6. _____

Name _____ Date _____

Building Vocabulary: Predictions

How do you predict these words will be used in the selection "From the Diary of Sir Isaac Newton"? Write your answers in the second column. Next, read the article. Then, clarify your answers in the third column.

Word	My prediction for how the word will be used	How the word was actually used
oval		
gravity		
credit		
succeeded		

Writing: Diary Entry

Suppose you are Sir Isaac Newton visiting the modern world.
What discoveries might surprise you? List some of them here.

1. _____

2. _____

3. _____

4. _____

5. _____

**Now write a diary entry in the voice of Newton that tells
about his thoughts of two or three of these discoveries. Use
what you know about Newton from the diary entries and your
own life to help you put together ideas.**

_____

_____

_____

_____

_____

_____

_____

_____

Name _____ Date _____

Building Vocabulary: Words with Multiple Meanings

Write two definitions for each word below.

Word	First Definition	Second Definition
credit	recognition	an amount of money placed at a person's disposal by a bank
close		
fly		
down		
fast		
space		

Name _____ Date _____

Building Vocabulary: Dictionary Definitions

Read the words and the definitions below. Write the word next to its definition. Use the magazine selections for context help.

nebula	**universe**	**inspected**	**artifacts**
sphere	**cosmic**	**exhibits**	

_____ objects made by humans, especially objects with historic or cultural interest

_____ relating to the whole universe, or cosmos

_____ displays of objects related to a topic

_____ examined carefully or officially

_____ a region or cloud of interstellar dust and gas that appears as a bright or dark patch in the sky

_____ any object similar in shape to a ball

_____ all the matter and space that exists, as a whole

Now choose two words. Tell how you used context to confirm that you matched the word with the correct definition.

_____

_____

_____

_____

_____

_____

Name _____ Date _____

Writing: A Memoir

A memoir tells about a special event or trip from a personal point of view. Write your own memoir. Start with a topic sentence that names the event. Then list what you did in order. End with a conclusion that tells how you felt about the event.

_____

_____

_____

_____

_____

_____

_____

_____

_____

_____

_____

_____

_____

_____

_____

Building Vocabulary: Word Associations

Choose two words from the vocabulary list below. Think about what you already know about each word. Then answer the following questions.

nebula	universe	inspected	artifacts
sphere	cosmic	exhibits	

Word _____

What do you think about when you read this word? _____

_____

Who might use this word? _____

_____

What do you already know about this word? _____

_____

Word _____

What do you think about when you read this word? _____

_____

Who might use this word? _____

_____

What do you already know about this word? _____

_____

Building Vocabulary: Knowledge Rating Chart

Show your knowledge of each word by adding information
to the other boxes in the row.

Word	Define or Use in a Sentence	Where Have I Seen or Heard It?	How Is It Used in the Selection?	Looks Like (Words or Sketch)
ancient				
constellations				
myths				
resented				
cloak				
boar				
Minotaur				

Writing: Description for Visualizing

Which one of Hercules' labors could you visualize best? Describe that labor below. Then draw a picture to show what you "saw" in your mind.

The labor I could visualize best was _____

_____

_____

Some details I "saw" in my mind include _____

_____

_____

Now draw what you visualized.

Building Vocabulary: Homophones

Read the homophone pairs. Write a definition for each word.

Homophone Pair	Definition
boar bore	a male pig something that lacks interest
fowl foul	

Write a homophone for each word. Then write a definition for each word.

Homophone Pair	Definition
herd	
maze	
deer	
right	
won	
great	

Name _____ Date _____

Building Vocabulary: Using Context to Understand a Word

Choose a word from any selection in the magazine that you can define in context. Answer the questions about the word.

My Word in Context: _____

I think this word means _____

_____

because _____

_____

_____

_____

_____

My word is _____

_____

My word is not _____

_____

Where else might I find this word? _____

_____

What makes this an important word to know? _____

_____

_____

_____

Writing: Opinion Paragraph

Would you like to travel in space? Why or why not? Write a paragraph stating your opinion and your reasons.

Main Idea:

Details (reasons):

Conclusion (strongest reason):

Name _____ Date _____

Reviewing Vocabulary: Word Search

Find and circle 13 words you learned about space. Work
with a partner to talk about what the words mean.

C	R	O	E	T	E	M	L	W	Y	E	W	J	I	A
C	O	M	M	A	N	D	E	R	O	L	X	J	H	R
W	C	N	O	B	G	R	A	V	I	T	Y	B	A	T
B	R	G	S	S	I	M	U	L	A	T	O	R	B	I
D	A	K	S	T	N	H	Q	J	P	N	S	I	I	F
E	T	F	A	N	E	R	E	H	P	S	O	M	T	A
P	E	X	T	P	E	L	L	S	E	O	U	S	A	C
L	R	O	E	O	R	L	L	R	T	R	G	T	T	
O	S	K	L	J	I	J	T	A	N	E	B	U	L	A
Y	G	O	L	O	N	H	C	E	T	H	V	U	H	R
G	Y	F	I	N	G	A	M	A	K	I	F	I	C	F
P	X	L	T	I	P	O	R	B	I	T	O	F	N	V
O	V	C	E	V	M	C	I	M	S	O	C	N	U	U
Y	R	W	P	H	V	Q	C	T	U	A	Q	R	A	S
C	X	L	Z	Z	Q	S	P	H	E	R	E	R	L	U

Words: artifact   deploy   nebula   sphere

commander   engineering   orbit

constellation   gravity   satellite

craters   habitat   simulator

Name _____ Date _____

Building Vocabulary: Word Associations

Think about what you already know about each word. Then
answer the questions for each word.

Word _____ **calving** _____

What do you think about when you read this word? _____

_____

Who might use this word? _____

_____

What do you already know about this word? _____

_____

Word _____ **currents** _____

What do you think about when you read this word? _____

_____

Who might use this word? _____

_____

What do you already know about this word? _____

_____

Now watch for these words in the magazine selection. Were you on the right track?

Writing: 5Ws

Use the 5Ws chart to help you organize keys ideas for a summary of a section of "Iceberg!" Your summary might tell how icebergs are formed or might tell about the Ross Ice Shelf iceberg. You can write your summary on page 81.

5Ws	Details from "Iceberg!"
Who studies the topic?	
What happens or happened?	
Where does or did it happen?	
When does or did it happen?	
Why does or did it happen?	

Name _____ Date _____

Writing: Summary

Now write a summary for the section of "Iceberg!" you chose.
Remember to use your notes from the 5Ws chart on page 80
to help you.

_____

_____

_____

_____

_____

_____

_____

_____

_____

_____

_____

_____

_____

_____

_____

_____

Building Vocabulary: Words with Multiple Meanings

Write two definitions for each word below.

Word	First Definition	Second Definition
calving	the process of a piece of glacier breaking off to form an iceberg	the process of a mother cow giving birth to a calf
view		
ship		
edges		

Name _____ Date _____

Building Vocabulary: Predictions

How do you predict these words will be used in the selection
"Cool Art"? Write your answers in the second column. Next, read
the article. Then, clarify your answers in the third column.

Word	My prediction for how the word will be used	How the word was actually used
sculptor		
entry		
chefs		

Now predict how this word will be used in "Experiment with Water
and Ice."

Word	My prediction for how the word will be used	How the word was actually used
hypothesis		

Writing: 5Ws

Write a news article about one of the festivals you read about in "Cool Art." First, use the 5Ws chart to help you organize your thoughts. Then write the article on page 85.

5Ws	Details from "Cool Art"
Who is involved with the festival?	
What is the festival?	
Where does or did the festival happen?	
When does or did the festival happen?	
Why does or did the festival happen?	

Writing: News Article

Use the 5Ws chart from page 84 to write a news article about
a festival from the selection "Cool Art."

_____

_____

_____

_____

_____

_____

_____

_____

_____

_____

_____

_____

_____

_____

_____

_____

Building Vocabulary: Concept Ladder

Answer the questions to complete the concept ladder. Write words or phrases to record your responses.

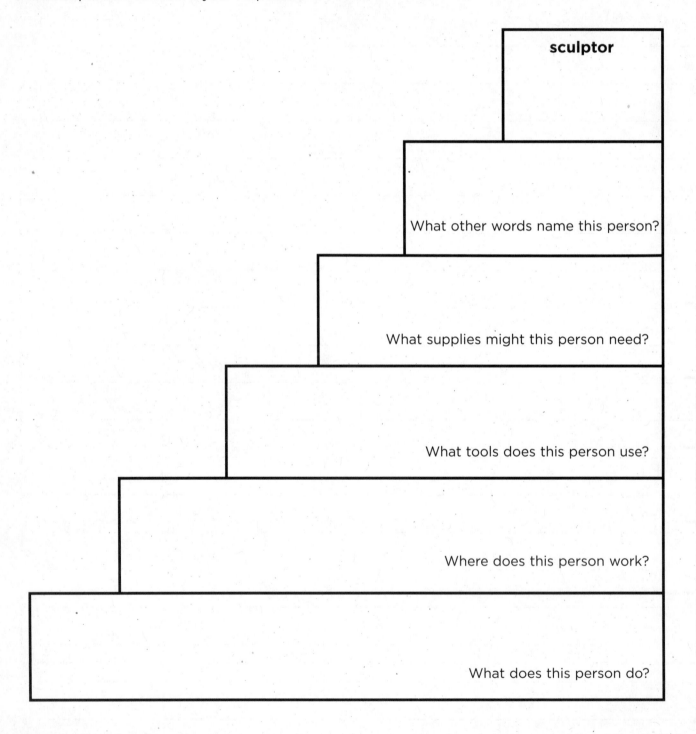

sculptor

What other words name this person?

What supplies might this person need?

What tools does this person use?

Where does this person work?

What does this person do?

Name _____ Date _____

Building Vocabulary: Knowledge Rating Chart

Show your knowledge of each word or phrase by adding
information to the other boxes in the row.

Word	Define or Use in a Sentence	Where Have I Seen or Heard It?	How Is It Used in the Selection?	Looks Like (Words or Sketch)
soggy				
adaptation				
carbon dioxide				
limp				
marsh				
knees				
moisture				
transpiration				

Water • Water Plant, Desert Plant *and* Seagulls and Whales

Writing: Main Idea Organizer

Choose a part of the selection to retell. Use the chart below to organize your thoughts. Write the details first. They will help you figure out the main idea and conclusion. Then retell your section to a partner.

Main Idea:

Detail:	**Detail:**	**Detail:**

Conclusion:

Building Vocabulary: Word Relationships

Choose four other word pairs to show more word relationships.
Arrange your words so that they are ranked by graduated
degrees of relationship. Possible word pairs include
tiny/enormous, *hot/cold*, and *ounce/gallon*.

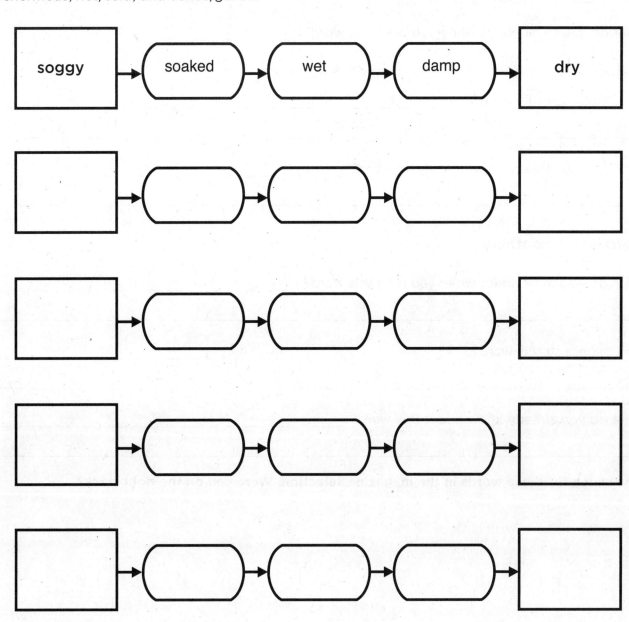

Building Vocabulary: Making Associations

Think about what you already know about the words
listed. Then answer the following questions.

Word _____ **yakking** _____

What do you think about when you read this word? _____

_____

Who might use this word? _____

_____

What do you already know about this word? _____

_____

Word _____ **soothing** _____

What do you think about when you read this word? _____

_____

Who might use this word? _____

_____

What do you already know about this word? _____

_____

Now watch for these words in the magazine selection. Were you on the right track?

Name _____ Date _____

Writing: A Friendly Letter

Write a letter to a friend. Tell what you learned about kayaks and kayaking. Draw a picture, if you like.

_____

_____

_____

Dear _____ ,

_____

_____

_____

_____

_____

_____

_____

_____

_____

_____

Building Vocabulary: Synonym Chart

Look at the two vocabulary words shown in the chart. Read the sentences around the word in "Yakking with a Kayaker." List a synonym from the interview for each word. Then think of other synonyms (words with similar meanings) for each word. Use a thesaurus if you need help.

Vocabulary Word	Synonyms
yakking	**1. talking** **2.** **3.**
soothing	**1. calming** **2.** **3.**

Now choose one of these words from the interview. Write it in the box. Then list synonyms for the word you chose.

narrow	build
walk	fast

Word	Synonyms
	1. 2. 3.

Name _____ . _____ Date _____

Building Vocabulary: Making Associations

Choose two vocabulary words. Think about what you already know
about each word. Then answer the following questions for
each word.

tsunami	swayed
swift	linen

Word _____

What do you think about when you read this word? _____

_____

Who might use this word? _____

_____

What do you already know about this word? _____

_____

Word _____

What do you think about when you read this word? _____

_____

Who might use this word? _____

_____

What do you already know about this word? _____

_____

Now watch for these words in the selection. Were you on the right track?

Writing: Notes for Visualizing

Which part of the selection could you visualize best? Describe
that part below. Then draw a picture to show what you "saw"
in your mind.

The part I could visualize best was _____

_____

_____

Some details I "saw" in my mind include _____

_____

_____

_____

Now draw what you visualized.

Name _____ Date _____

Building Vocabulary: Homophones

Complete each homophone pair. Then write a definition for each
word in the pair.

Homophones	Definitions
swayed suede	swung from side to side soft leather
seen	
ate	
way	
rode	

© Great Source. Copying is permitted; see page ii.

Building Vocabulary: Predictions

How do you predict these words will be used in "A Man for All Seas"? Write your answers in the second column. Next, read the article. Then clarify your answers in the third column.

Word	My prediction for how the word will be used	How the word was actually used
wreck		
oceanographer		
submersible		
vents		
plaque		
footage		

Name _____ Date _____

Writing: Journal Entry

What might Robert Ballard have written in a journal entry when he discovered the *Titanic*? Write a journal entry about it in the space below. Use what you know from the article and your own life to help you put together ideas.

September 1, 1985

_____

_____

_____

_____

_____

_____

_____

_____

_____

_____

_____

_____

_____

_____

_____

Building Vocabulary: Words with Multiple Meanings

Write two definitions for each word below.

Word	First Definition	Second Definition
plaque	a flat piece of metal, wood, or stone with writing on it to honor a person or an event	a film on tooth surfaces that hardens and attracts decay-causing bacteria
floor		
program		
float		
pools		

Building Vocabulary: Synonym and Antonym Chart

For the word *detach*, write three words that are synonyms
(similar in meaning). Then, write three words that are antonyms
(opposite in meaning). Next, repeat the process for two other
words you choose from the article.

Word	Synonyms	Antonyms
detach	1. remove 2. 3.	1. attach 2. 3.
	1. 2. 3.	1. 2. 3.
	1. 2. 3.	1. 2. 3.

Writing: Notes for Visualizing

Which home were you able to visualize best? Describe the home below. Use as many details as you can from the text. Then draw a picture of how you imagined it in your mind.

The part I could visualize best was _____

_____

_____

Some details I "saw" in my mind include _____

_____

_____

Now draw what you visualized.

Building Vocabulary: Words with *Auto*

Write examples and meanings of words with the combining form *auto* in the chart. One answer is given.

auto means "self, alone"

Word	Definition
1. automatic	something that is regulated by itself
2.	
3.	
4.	
5.	

Building Vocabulary: Word Associations

Choose two vocabulary words. Think about what you already know about each word. Then answer the questions for each word.

scuba diving	valve
trio	marina

Word ....

What do you think about when you read this word? ....

....

Who might use this word? ....

....

What do you already know about this word? ....

....

Word ....

What do you think about when you read this word? ....

....

Who might use this word? ....

....

What do you already know about this word? ....

....

Now watch for these words in the magazine selection. Were you on the right track?

Writing: Story Organizer

Complete the story organizer to help you organize details and events from "Underwater Hotel."

Characters:

Setting:

Title:

Plot:

Writing: Book Jacket

If "Underwater Hotel" were a book, it would have a book jacket to tell readers something about it. Use the story organizer on page 103 to write a book jacket for "Underwater Hotel." Include the title, the main characters, the setting, and a little about the plot (but not the ending).

_____

_____

_____

_____

_____

_____

_____

_____

_____

_____

_____

_____

_____

_____

Building Vocabulary: Using Context to Understand a Word

Select a vocabulary word or other word from the story that you defined from the context. Complete the statements and answer the questions about your word.

| scuba diving | valve |
| trio | marina |

My Word in Context:

I think this word means _____

_____

_____

because _____

_____

My word is _____

My word is not _____

Where else might I find this word? _____

What makes this an important word to know? _____

_____

_____

Name .... Date ....

Building Vocabulary: Using a Word Map

Write your definition of *suspense* in the top box. After reading
the selection, change your definition if you need to. Then answer
the questions.

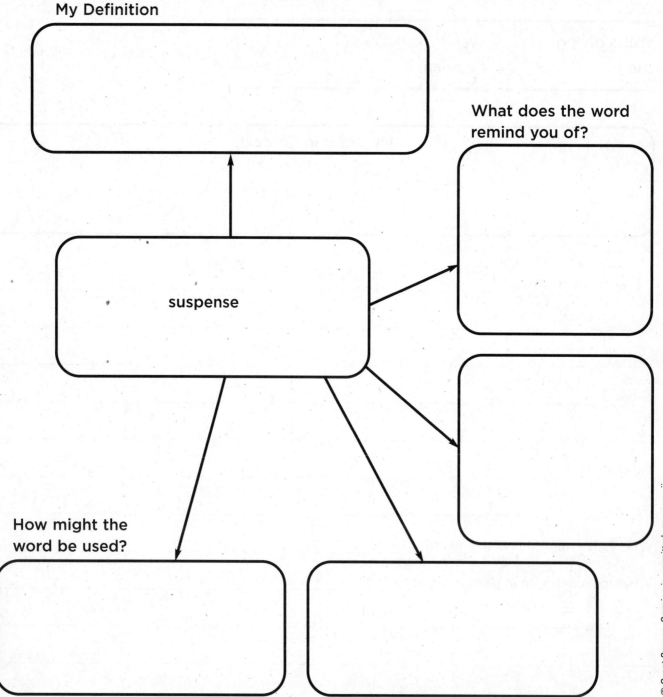

My Definition

**What does the word
remind you of?**

suspense

**How might the
word be used?**

Name .... Date ....

Writing: Notes for Visualizing

Which part of the play were you able to visualize best? Describe it below. Use as many details as you can from the text. Then draw a picture of how you imagined that part in your mind.

The part I could visualize best was _____

_____

_____

Some details I "saw" in my mind include _____

_____

_____

Now draw what you visualized.

Building Vocabulary: Words with Multiple Meanings

Write two definitions for each word below.

Word	First Definition	Second Definition
slick	smart, clever, or tricky	smooth, glossy, or oily
tank		
locks		
bands		
line		

Name _____ Date _____

Building Vocabulary: A Word Web

Write the word *platform* or *fumes* in the center oval.
Write the definition in the bottom box. After you read
the selection, add details around the oval that help
define the word.

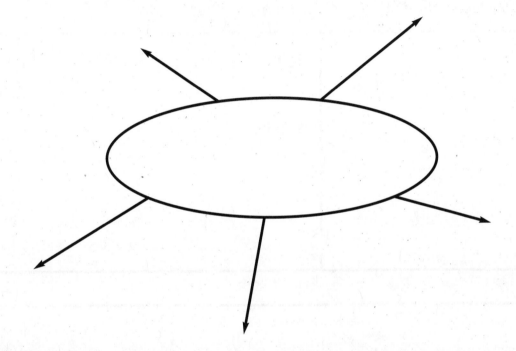

Write the complete definition here:

Writing: Point of View

Think about the point of view expressed by each of the two authors in "Oil and Water: Two Points of View." Write a sentence or two to identify each point of view. Next, write details from the essay to support each point of view. Then, write your own opinion about the issue of offshore drilling for oil.

Drilling at Sea: We Need the Oil	Drilling at Sea: Too Dangerous
Point of View: **Details:**	**Point of View:** **Details:**

My Opinion:

Reasons:

Building Vocabulary: Words with Multiple Meanings

Write two definitions for each word below.

Word	First Definition	Second Definition
fumes	irritating gases	lets off one's rage
platform		
drill		
place		
rigs		

Building Vocabulary: Making Associations

Think about what you already know about the two words listed.
Then answer the following questions for each word.

Word _____insignificant_____

What do you think about when you read this word? _____

_____

Who might use this word? _____

_____

What do you already know about this word? _____

_____

Word _____enraged_____

What do you think about when you read this word? _____

_____

Who might use this word? _____

_____

What do you already know about this word? _____

_____

Now watch for these words in the magazine selection. Were you on the right track?

Writing: Somebody Wanted But So

Use this chart to help you organize your thoughts for a
summary of "Uncle Toad Saves the World."

	My Notes
Somebody (an important character)	
Wanted (a key problem with details)	
But (conflict for the character)	
So (an outcome)	

Now write a summary of the tale.

_____

_____

_____

_____

_____

_____

_____

_____

Building Vocabulary: Prefix *en-*

Write words you know that contain the prefix *en-*. Write a definition for each word. Use a dictionary to help you, if you wish. One answer is given.

---

en- means "in," "into," "make," "make into," "make like"

Words	Definitions
1. enlarge	**to make larger**
2.	
3.	
4.	
5.	

Building Vocabulary: Writing Riddles

Show that you know what *riddle* means. Write three riddles.
You can write ones you already know, or you can make up
new ones.

1. _____

_____

_____

_____

_____

_____

2. _____

_____

_____

_____

_____

_____

3. _____

_____

_____

_____

_____

Writing: Notes for Visualizing

Which riddle on page 62 of the magazine could you visualize better?
Write details that you would include in a funny picture to go with the
riddle. Then draw a picture to show what you "saw" in your mind.

The riddle I could visualize better was ....

....

....

Some details I "saw" in my mind include ....

....

....

....

Now draw what you visualized.

Building Vocabulary: Synonym and Antonym Chart

Write any words you wish in the first column. Think of three other words that are synonyms (similar in meaning) for each word you write. Then think of three words that are antonyms (opposites) for each word. Use a thesaurus to help you.

Word	Synonyms	Antonyms
	1. 2. 3.	1. 2. 3.
	1. 2. 3.	1. 2. 3.
	1. 2. 3.	1. 2. 3.

Building Vocabulary: Using a Word Map

Write a vocabulary word in the center box. Write a definition.
Next, read the selection. Then answer the questions.

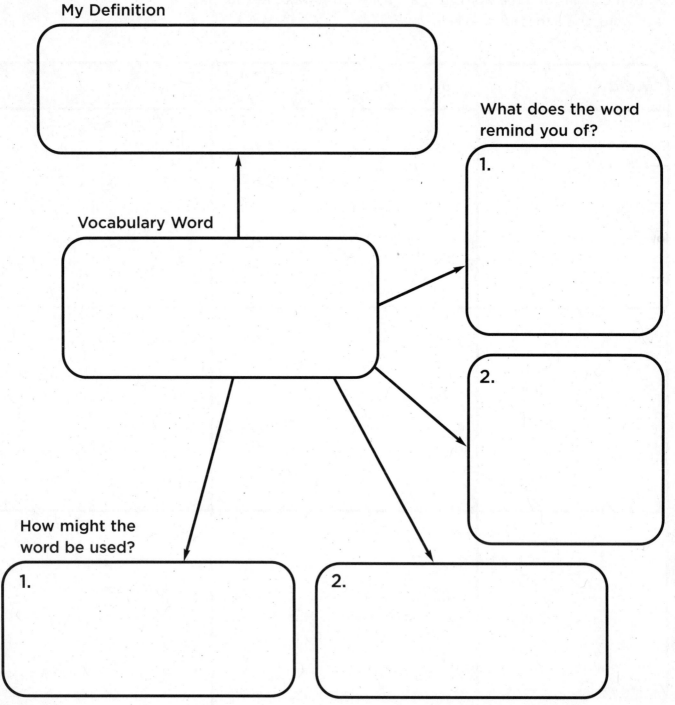

My Definition

Vocabulary Word

What does the word remind you of?

1.

2.

How might the word be used?

1.

2.

Name _____ Date _____

Writing: Notes for Visualizing

What part of Machu Picchu could you visualize best? Describe the part below. Then draw a picture of how you imagined it in your mind.

The part I could visualize best was _____

_____

_____

Some details I "saw" in my mind include _____

_____

_____

Now draw what you visualized.

Building Vocabulary: Words with Multiple Meanings

Write two definitions for each word below.

Word	First Definition	Second Definition
terrace	a porch or walkway	a raised bank of earth used for planting
towers		
ruler		
ruins		

Name _____ Date _____

Building Vocabulary: Predictions

How do you predict these words will be used in "Washington, D.C.—The Birth of a City"? Write your answers in the second column. Next, read the play. Then, clarify your answers in the third column.

Word	My prediction for how the word will be used	How the word was actually used
donated		
architect		
remodeling		
bold		
Congress		
precise		

Summarize: Somebody Wanted But So

Use this chart to help you organize your thoughts for a summary of "Washington, D.C.—The Birth of a City." After you fill in the chart, use your notes to write a paragraph that summarizes the play.

	My Notes
Somebody (an important character)	
Wanted (a key problem with details)	
But (conflict for the character)	
So (an outcome)	

Now write your paragraph.

_____

_____

_____

_____

_____

_____

Building Vocabulary: Synonym and Antonym Chart

Think of two or three other words that are synonyms (similar in meaning) for each word in the first column. Next, think of two or three words that are antonyms (opposite in meaning) for each word in the first column. Use a thesaurus to help you.

Vocabulary Word	Synonyms	Antonyms
donated	1. given 2. 3.	1. taken 2. 3.
bold	1. 2. 3.	1. 2. 3.
precise	1. 2. 3.	1. 2. 3.

Building Vocabulary: Making Associations

Pick two words from the vocabulary list below. Think about what you already know about each word. Then answer the following questions for each word.

mural	panels	customs
Aztec	suffered	

Word _____

What do you think about when you read this word? _____

_____

Who might use this word? _____

_____

What do you already know about this word? _____

_____

Word _____

What do you think about when you read this word? _____

_____

Who might use this word? _____

_____

What do you already know about this word? _____

_____

Now watch for these words in the magazine selection. Were you on the right track?

Writing: Main Idea Chart

Choose one part of "City Walls That Talk" to retell. Fill in the
chart for just that part of the article. Write the details first. They
will help you figure out the main idea and conclusion. Then use
the chart to retell your part.

Main Idea:

Detail:	Detail:	Detail:

Conclusion:

Building Vocabulary: Illustrated Mini-Dictionary

Choose three words for an illustrated mini-dictionary. Write a definition and then make an illustration for each word.

mural	customs	Aztecs
suffered	panel	

Vocabulary Word	Definition	Illustration

Building Vocabulary: Using a Word Map

Write a vocabulary word in the center box. Write a definition.
Next read the selection. Then answer the questions.

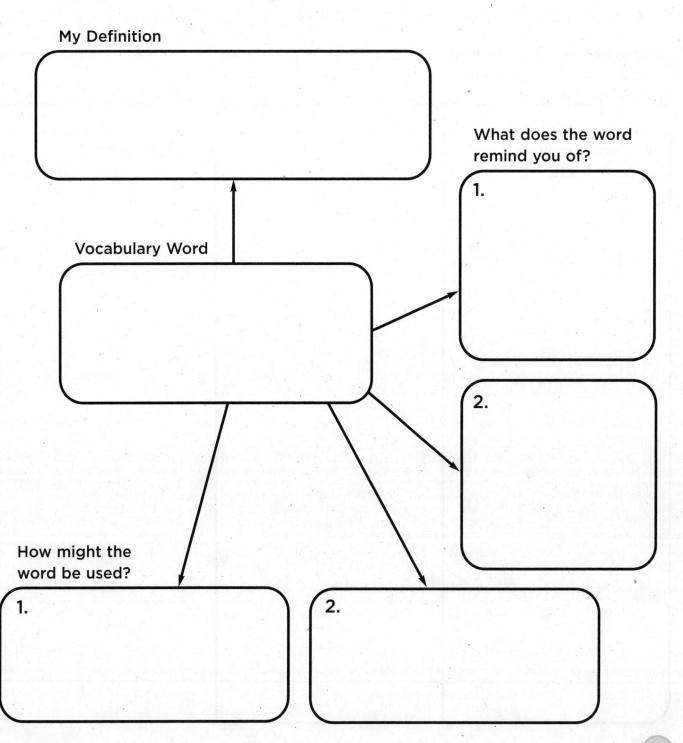

My Definition

What does the word remind you of?

1.

2.

Vocabulary Word

How might the word be used?

1.

2.

Name _____ Date _____

Writing: Indoor Sport Chart

Choose one indoor sport that interested you. On the chart, record your ideas about what is involved in playing that sport and what it is like to participate in that sport.

Indoor Sport:		
Type of equipment needed to play the sport indoors:	**Type of room needed:**	**What it is like to play the sport indoors:**

Writing: Description of an Indoor Sport

Use the chart on page 128 to help you visualize the indoor
sport you chose. Next, draw a scene of the sport being played.
Then, write a description of what is happening in your illustration.

_____

_____

_____

_____

_____

_____

_____

Building Vocabulary: Words within a Word

How many words can you find in the word below? Write them in the chart.

TOURNAMENT

Two Letters	Three Letters	Four or More Letters
to	man	turn

Name _____ Date _____

Building Vocabulary: Knowledge Rating Chart

Show your knowledge of each word by adding information to the other boxes.

Word	Define or Use in a Sentence	Where Have I Seen or Heard It?	How Is It Used in the Selection?	Looks Like (Words or Sketch)
luxury				
quality				
urban				
economy				
pollution				

Writing: Fact and Opinion Chart

Fill in the chart below with facts and opinions from "City Greens." An example has been done for you. Remember, a fact can be proven. An opinion is how one person thinks or feels.

Fact	Opinion
More than 200 million Americans live in or near a city.	**Grass and trees are a welcome sight.**

Name _____ Date _____

Building Vocabulary: Synonym and Antonym Chart

Think of three words that could be synonyms (similar in meaning) for each word. Next, think of three words that could be antonyms (opposite in meaning) for each word. Use a thesaurus to help you.

Vocabulary Word	Synonyms	Antonyms
luxury	1. fancy 2. 3.	1. cheap 2. 3.
quality	1. 2. 3.	1. 2. 3.
pollution	1. 2. 3.	1. 2. 3.

Building Vocabulary: Predictions

How do you predict these words will be used in "Lost and Found in Chicago"? Write your answers in the second column. Next, read the story. Then, clarify your answers in the third column.

Word	My prediction for how the word will be used	How the word was actually used
long-winded		
midway		
grooming		
frantic		

Name _____ Date _____

Writing: Personal Experience

As you reflect on "Lost & Found in Chicago," think about an experience you have had in an unfamiliar setting. Describe how you felt being in a new place. Use the lines below to write a paragraph telling about your experience.

_____

_____

_____

_____

_____

_____

_____

_____

_____

_____

_____

_____

_____

_____

_____

Building Vocabulary: Illustrated Mini-Dictionary

Write a definition and then make an illustration for each
vocabulary word.

Vocabulary Word	Definition	Illustration
long-winded		
midway		
grooming		
frantic		

Building Vocabulary: Making Associations

Pick two words from the vocabulary list below. Think about what you already know about each word. Then answer the following questions for each word.

major	conflicts	opportunity
ethnic	determined	mourned

Word _____

What do you think about when you read this word? _____

_____

Who might use this word? _____

_____

What do you already know about this word? _____

_____

Word _____

What do you think about when you read this word? _____

_____

Who might use this word? _____

_____

What do you already know about this word? _____

_____

Now watch for these words in the magazine selection. Were you on the right track?

Writing: Cause and Effect Chart

Fill in the following chart with information you gathered from reading "Mayor Tom Bradley." An example has been done for you.

Cause	Effect
Bradley had a hard childhood.	**He was determined to have a better life.**

Writing: Cause and Effect Paragraph

Read what you wrote in the chart on page 138. You might notice that a series of causes and effects tells a story. Using the causes and effects from your chart, write a paragraph that retells what you learned about the life of Tom Bradley.

_____

_____

_____

_____

_____

_____

_____

_____

_____

_____

_____

_____

_____

_____

_____

Building Vocabulary: Using Context

Choose three of the following vocabulary words to include in a mini-speech that you would give if you were running for public office. Define the words. Then write and perform your speech.

major	conflicts	opportunity
ethnic	determined	mourned

1. The word _____ means _____

_____

2. The word _____ means _____

_____

3. The word _____ means _____

_____

Use the lines below to write your mini-speech. When you finish, give your speech to the group.

_____

_____

_____

_____

_____

_____

_____

Name _____ Date _____

Building Vocabulary: Using a Word Map

Write a vocabulary word in the center box. Write a definition.
Next read the selection. Then answer the questions.

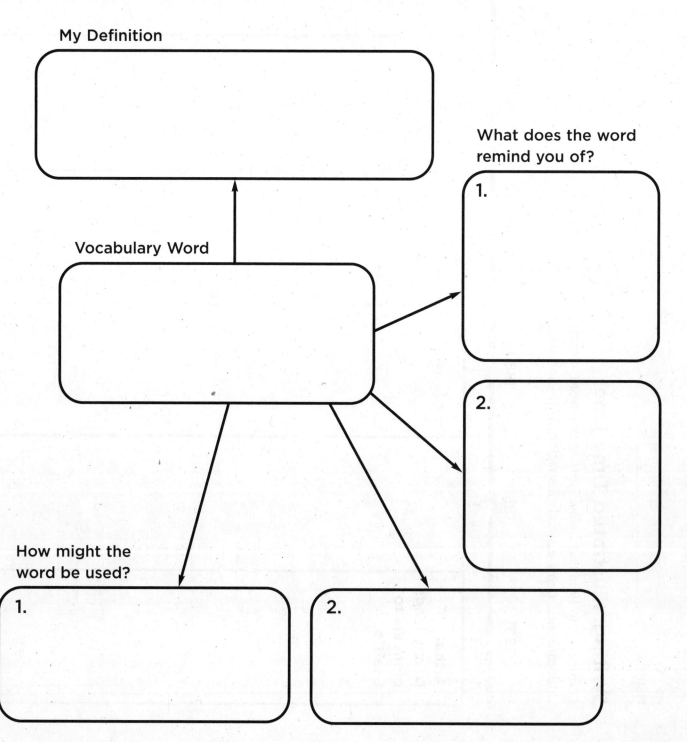

My Definition

Vocabulary Word

What does the word remind you of?

1.

2.

How might the word be used?

1.

2.

Writing: Illustrated Time Line

Complete the time line below with details from "Seattle Underground." Draw a small illustration with each time line entry.

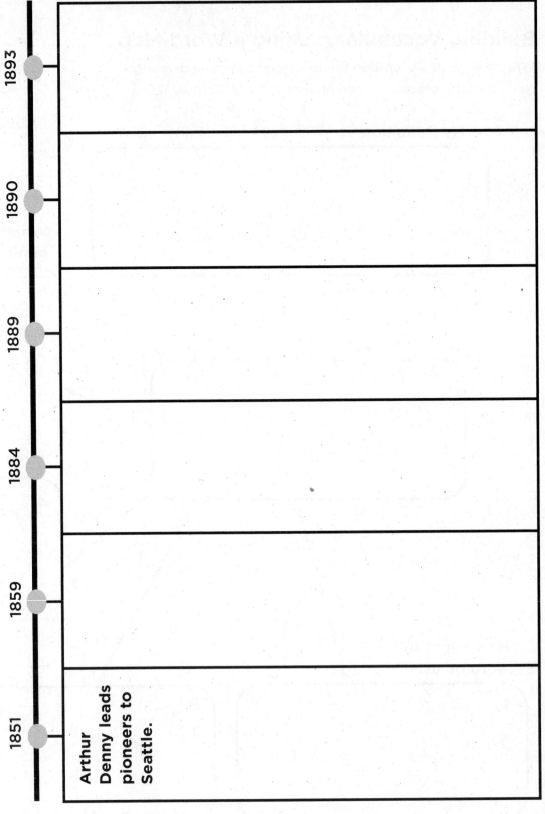

1851	1859	1884	1889	1890	1893

Arthur Denny leads pioneers to Seattle.

Building Vocabulary: Words with Multiple Meanings

What are two meanings for each of the words below? Write them in
the chart. Then choose your own word that has multiple meanings.
Write the definitions in the chart.

Word	First Definition	Second Definition
network	an interconnected system	a radio or television company
shady		
stalls		

Name _____   Date _____

Building Vocabulary: Knowledge Rating Chart

Show your knowledge of each word by adding information to the other boxes.

Word	Define or Use in a Sentence	Where Have I Seen or Heard It?	How Is It Used in the Selection?	Looks Like (Words or Sketch)
canals				
lagoon				
drastic				
forecast				
environ-mentalists				
cesspool				
inflate				

Writing: 5Ws

The 5Ws—*who*, *what*, *where*, *when*, and *why*—give readers the basic information about what happens in an article. What do the 5Ws tell you about "Can a Sinking City Be Saved?" Fill in the chart below.

5Ws	Details from "Can a Sinking City Be Saved?"
What is the article about?	
Who is affected in the article?	
Where does the article take place?	
When do the major events of the article take place?	
Why is this topic important?	

Building Vocabulary: News Report

Write a brief news report about the problem facing the city of
Venice. Use three (or more) vocabulary words in your report.

canals	drastic	environmentalists	inflate
lagoon	forecast	cesspool	

_____

_____

_____

_____

_____

_____

_____

_____

_____

_____

_____

_____

**When you finish writing your news report, read it aloud to a partner. How are your reports
similar and different?**

Building Vocabulary: Predictions

How do you predict these words will be used in "Insect Cities"?
Write your answers in the second column. Next, read the article.
Then, clarify your answers in the third column.

Word	My prediction for how the word will be used	How the word was actually used
social		
colony		
castes		
chambers		
cells		
pollen		
nectar		

Writing: Draw and Label an Ant City

Draw a detailed diagram of an ant city. Include the labels of the various workers and locations.

Be sure to include:

1. nursery

2. queen's chamber

3. storage chamber

4. workers' rest chamber

5. queen

6. males

7. workers

Building Vocabulary: Words with Multiple Meanings

Write two definitions for each word below.

Word	First Definition	Second Definition
cells	small compartments	rooms in a prison or jail
care		
trunk		
spring		

Building Vocabulary: Making Associations

Pick two words from the vocabulary list below. Think about what you already know about each word. Then answer the following questions for each word.

mortals	harvests	theories
noble	fascinated	spark

Word _____

What do you think about when you read this word? _____

_____

Who might use this word? _____

_____

What do you already know about this word? _____

_____

Word _____

What do you think about when you read this word? _____

_____

Who might use this word? _____

_____

What do you already know about this word? _____

_____

Now watch for these words in the magazine selection. Were you on the right track?

Name _____ Date _____

Writing: Main Idea Chart

First, choose whether you are going to write about the section on Atlantis or El Dorado. Next, in the chart below, write three details about the section you chose. Then, figure out the main idea and write it in the top section. Finally, use the information in the chart to come up with a logical conclusion. Write it in the bottom part of the chart.

Main Idea:

Detail:	**Detail:**	**Detail:**

Conclusion:

Now retell the section you wrote about to a partner. Does your partner have any questions?

Building Vocabulary: Words with Multiple Meanings

Write two definitions for each word below.

Word	First Definition	Second Definition
spark	hot, glowing matter	to set in motion
covered		
capital		
legend		
subject		

Writing: Compare and Contrast Chart

Fill in the chart below with details that compare and contrast each of the three cities mentioned in "Urban Transportation." Add your city or town to the end of the chart, and add details about your local transportation system.

City	Transportation Details
Los Angeles	
San Francisco	
New York	

Writing: Compare and Contrast Paragraph

Choose two cities from the chart on page 153. Using the information you recorded in the chart, write a paragraph that compares and contrasts the public transportation in those cities.

_____

_____

_____

_____

_____

_____

_____

_____

_____

_____

_____

_____

_____

_____

_____

_____

Building Vocabulary: Words within a Word

How many words can you find in the word below? Write them in the chart.

TRANSPORTATION

Two Letters	Three Letters	Four or More Letters
to	ran	port

The Reading Process

The Reading Process has three parts: Before Reading, During Reading, and After Reading.

BEFORE Reading

Preview the Material

Look over the selection before you read. Does the selection look like a short story or other fiction? If so, look at the title, introduction, or illustrations. Does the selection look like nonfiction? If so, look for headings, boldfaced words, photos, or captions. Also, ask yourself how the information is organized. Is the author comparing or contrasting information about the topic? Is the information presented in a sequence using signal words like *first, second, third*, or *finally*? Understanding how the author is presenting information will help you to recognize key information as you read.

Make Predictions

When you make predictions, you actively connect with the words on the page. Think about what you already know about the subject or anything you see. Then think of yourself as a text detective, putting together what you know with new details in the text. Predict what you think will happen, why an event caused something to happen, or what might come next in a series of events. Then double-check what you have read to confirm or support your predictions. Did your prediction match the text? If not, use what you have learned to revise your prediction and keep on reading.

Set a Purpose

Begin by reviewing what do you already know about the topic or situation in the text. Then think about what you want to find out.

Questions to Ask Yourself Before *Reading:*

- Before I read this material, what do I think it is going to be about?

- After looking through the article, what do I already know about this subject?

- What should I be thinking about as I read?

Engage with the text

As your eyes look at the words, your brain should be working to make connections between the words and what you already know. Have you had an experience similar to one that a character is having? Do you know someone like the character? Have you read another book about the topic? You will also want to connect what you read to the predictions you made before reading. Confirm, revise, predict again is a cycle that continues until the reading material is completed. All of these questions will go on inside your head. Sometimes, though, it helps to think out loud or write.

Monitor your understanding

As you read, stop from time to time and ask yourself, "Do I understand what I just read?" If the text doesn't make sense, there are several steps you can take.

- Go back and reread the text carefully.
- Read on to see if more information helps you understand.
- Pull together the author's ideas in a summary.
- Retell, or say in your own words, the events that have happened.
- Picture in your mind what the author described.
- Look for context clues or word-structure clues to help you figure out hard words.

This takes some practice. Remember, to be a successful reader, you must be an active reader. Make an effort to check your understanding every so often when you read a new selection.

Questions to Ask Yourself While Reading:

- As I am reading, what important details am I finding?
- Which of these ideas seem to be the most important?
- Does this information fit with anything I already know?
- What do I see in my mind as I read this material?
- Do I understand the information in the charts or tables? Does it help me to understand what I am reading?

AFTER Reading

Summarize

Reread to locate the most important ideas in the story or article.

Respond and Reflect

Talk with a partner about what you have read. What did you learn from the text? What questions do you have? Talking about reading helps you understand better what you have read.

Ask Questions

Try asking yourself questions that begin like this:
Can I compare or contrast? . . . evaluate?   . . . connect?   . . . examine?
                                    . . . analyze?   . . . relate?

Engage with the Text

Good readers engage with the text all the time, even when they have finished reading. When you tie events in your life or something else you have read to what you are currently reading, you become more involved with your reading. In the process, you are learning more about your values, relationships in your family, and problems in the world around you.

Questions to Ask Yourself After *Reading*:

- Have I learned something that makes me want to change the way I think about this topic?
- What was this article about?
- Are there parts of this material that I really want to remember?
- What was the author trying to tell me?

Glossary

A

adaptation (ad ap TAY shun) *noun.* the ability to adjust to one's surroundings

advantage (ad VAN tidge) *noun.* something that improves one's position

air pressure (AIR PRESH ur) *noun.* the weight of air pressing down on an object

alias (AIL ee uhss) *noun.* an assumed name used to conceal one's identity

altar (ALL tur) *noun.* a raised place where religious services are performed

ambush (AM bush) *noun.* a surprise attack from a hidden position

ancestors (AN sess turs) *noun.* family members who lived at an earlier time

ancient (AIN shent) *adjective.* of or relating to times long past

archaeologists (ar kee OL uh jists) *noun.* scientists who dig for and study objects from the past

architect (AR kuh tekt) *noun.* a person who designs and draws plans for buildings

artifacts (AR tuh fakts) *noun.* objects made or shaped by human craft

atmosphere (AT muss feer) *noun.* the gaseous mass surrounding the earth

automatic (aw tuh MAT ik) *adjective.* able to operate without the control of a human being

Aztec (AZ tek) *noun.* people who had a great civilization in central Mexico during the sixteenth century

B

boar (boor) *noun.* a male pig

bold (bold) *adjective.* different and daring; standing out from others

breeding grounds (BREE ding groundz) *noun.* a place where animals give birth to or hatch their young

briefing (BREE fing) *noun.* a meeting at which instructions or preparatory information is given

C

calving (KAV ing) *verb.* separating into smaller pieces of ice

canals (kuh NALS) *noun.* long, narrow passages for ships to travel through

carbon dioxide (KAR ben dy OK side) *noun.* a gas in the air that is used by plants

carve (karv) *verb.* to cut into a desired shape

castes (kasts) *noun.* specialized levels in colonies of social insects, such as ants

cells (selz) *noun.* tiny rooms

ceremonies (SAIR uh moan eez) *noun.* acts or rituals done for special events

cesspool (SESS pool) *noun.* an underground container used to hold waste from toilets and sinks; an unhealthy, smelly place

chambers (CHAIM burz) *noun.* rooms

chant (chant) *noun.* a song that can be sung or spoken over and over

chariots (CHAIR ee utz) *noun.* ancient, two-wheeled carts pulled by horses

charter (CHAR tur) *noun.* a written document issued by a ruler or government

chefs (shefz) *noun.* skilled cooks who manage restaurant kitchens

cloak (kloke) *noun.* a loose outer garment, such as a cape

colony (KOL uh nee) *noun.* a group of people who settle in a distant territory but remain subject to or closely associated with the parent country

commander (kuh MAN dur) *noun.* a person who gives orders

communication (kuh myoo nuh KAY shun) *noun.* the exchange of thoughts, messages, or information

complicated (KOM pluh kay ted) *adjective.* not easy

conflicts (KON flikts) *noun*. fights, disagreements

congestion (kun JEST shun) *noun*. overcrowding

congress (KONG gress) *noun*. the group of people who make laws for a country

constellations (kon stuh LAY shuns) *noun*. formations of stars perceived as figures or designs

cooped up (koopt up) *adjective*. confined to a small space

cosmic (KOZ mik) *adjective*. of or relating to the universe, as distinct from Earth

craters (KRAY terz) *noun*. bowl-shaped depressions in a surface made by an explosion or the impact of a body, such as a meteoroid

currents (KUR entz) *noun*. strong movements of water in the ocean

customs (KUSS temz) *noun*. the practices followed by people of a particular group or region

D

daring (DAIR ing) *noun*. boldness and courage; fearlessness

dense (denss) *adjective*. thick

deployed (dee PLOYD) *verb*. put into use or action

detach (dee TATCH) *verb*. separate, disconnect

determined (dee TUR muhnd) *adjective*. showing firmness of purpose

disgusted (diss GUSS tid) *adjective*. sickened

dissolve (dih ZOLV) *verb*. to change from a solid to a liquid

dock (dok) *verb*. to maneuver a vehicle into or next to a dock

dome (dohm) *noun*. a roof with a circular or elliptical base and a hemispherical shape

donated (DOH nay tid) *verb*. made a contribution to a fund or cause

drastic (DRASS tik) *adjective*. severe or radical in nature; extreme

drought (drout) *noun*. a long period without rain; dryness

E

echolocating (EK o lo kay ting) *verb*. making high-pitched sounds and listening to their echoes to determine the direction and distance of objects

economy (ih KON uh mee) *noun*. a system of managing money, goods, natural resources, and services

elementary (el uh MEN tuh ree) *adjective*. simple; not complicated

engineering (en juh NEER ing) *noun*. the application of scientific and mathematical ideas to practical purposes, such as the design of efficient machines

enraged (en RAJD) *adjective*. very angry

entry (EN tree) *noun*. something that is entered into a contest or race

environment (en VI ren ment) *noun*. the conditions that create one's surroundings

environmentalists (en vi ren MENT uh listz) *noun*. people who work to protect the environment

equator (ih KWAY tur) *noun*. an imaginary circle that divides the earth in half

ethnic (ETH nik) *adjective*. of or relating to a group of people who share language, culture, religion, race, or nation

exhibits (ig ZIB itz) *noun*. public displays

F

fabric (FAB rik) *noun*. cloth produced by knitting or weaving fibers

fascinated (FASS uh nay ted) *verb*. held the attention or interest of

flints (flintz) *noun.* hard quartz stones that are usually dull gray and produce sparks when struck against each other or against steel

foil (foil) *noun.* a thin, flexible sheet of metal

footage (FOOT idge) *noun.* an amount or length of film or videotape

forecast (FOR kast) *noun.* a prediction, as of coming events or conditions

foreground (FOR ground) *noun.* the part of the picture that seems closest to the viewer

forensics (fuh REN sikz) *noun.* the science of studying evidence to determine facts.

frantic (FRAN tik) *adjective.* wildly upset and worried

fumes (fyoomz) *noun.* smoke or gas that is unhealthy to breathe

funnel (FUN ul) *noun.* a tool with a narrow, open tube at one end, used to pour liquids into a container

G

generations (jen uh RAY shunz) *noun.* the offspring that come from common ancestors

gravity (GRAV uh tee) *noun.* the natural force of attraction exerted by Earth upon objects at or near its surface

grooming (GROOM ing) *verb.* cleaning and combing

gully (GUL ee) *noun.* a ditch cut by running water

H

habitats (HAB uh tatz) *noun.* structures that provide a controlled environment

harvest (HAR vist) *verb.* to gather a crop

harvests (HAR vistz) *noun.* the gathering of crops

historical district (hih STOR uh kul DIS trikt) *noun.* an area that is preserved and protected because it is an important record of history

hypothesis (hie POTH uh siss) *noun.* a statement of a possible explanation

I

ignite (ig NITE) *verb.* to set fire to

illusion (ih LOO zhen) *noun.* a false perception; an appearance that is not real

impressions (im PRESH enz) *noun.* marks produced on the surface by applying pressure

inflate (in FLAIT) *verb.* to increase in size by filling with air or a gas

insignificant (in sig NIFF uh kent) *adjective.* not important

inspected (in SPECT id) *verb.* examined carefully

J

jammed (jamd) *verb.* blocked or clogged

justify (JUSS tuh fie) *verb.* to prove to be right

K

kivas (KEE vuz) *noun.* underground chambers in a Pueblo village

knees (neez) *noun.* round or pointed protrusions on water-dwelling trees, such as cypress, that resemble human knees

L

lagoon (luh GOON) *noun.* a shallow lake that is partly cut off from the sea by a land form

launched (lawnchd) *verb.* thrust into motion

legends (LEDGE enz) *noun.* stories about a group's origin

lens (lenz) *noun.* a ground or molded piece of glass with opposite surfaces, either or both of which are curved

limp (limp) *adjective.* without firmness; droopy

linen (LIN un) *noun.* cloth items such as sheets, tablecloths, and napkins

loch (lok) *noun.* lake (Scottish)

long-winded (long WIN did) *adjective*. speaking or writing at great length; long and wordy

lowly (LOH lee) *adjective*. in an unimportant position

lunar module (LOO nur MOJ ul) *noun*. a spacecraft designed to take astronauts from a command module orbiting the moon to the lunar surface and back

luxury (LUG jor ree) *noun*. something that adds to a person's pleasure but is not necessary

M

magnify (MAG nuh fi) *verb*. to make larger

major (MAY jur) *adjective*. very important

maneuver (muh NOO ver) *verb*. to move from one position to another

marina (muh REE nuh) *noun*. a dock for boats that often has supplies and services, such as gas, food, and bathrooms

marsh (marsh) *noun*. an area of low, wet land covered with grasses and other similar plants

martian (MAR shen) *noun*. an imaginary creature that lives on Mars

mesa (MAY suh) *noun*. a flat-topped large hill or mountain with steep sides going down to flat land below

meteor (MEE tee ur) *noun*. a bright trail or streak that appears in the sky

midway (MID way) *noun*. the area of a fair, carnival, or circus where sideshows and other amusements are held

migrate (MI grate) *verb*. to move to a different region, especially at a particular time of year

minotaur (MIN uh tor) *noun*. a monster in Greek mythology who was half man and half bull

mission (MISH en) *noun*. an aerospace operation intended to carry out a specific objective

moisture (MOIS chur) *noun*. water or slight wetness in the air or on a surface

momentum (mo MEN tum) *noun*. the force of a physical object in motion

monitors (MON uh turz) *noun*. video displays that show information on a screen

mortals (MOR tulz) *noun*. human beings

mourned (mornd) *verb*. grieved for someone who died

mummy (MUM ee) *noun*. a dead body that has been prepared for burial in order to keep it in good condition

mural (MYOOR ul) *noun*. a large painting sometimes painted onto the outside wall of a building

musty (MUS tee) *adjective*. having a stale smell

myths (mithz) *noun*. traditional stories told in order to explain aspects of the natural world or the ideals of society

N

Navajo (NAV uh ho) *noun*. a Native American tribe that lives in Arizona, New Mexico, and Utah

nebula (NEB yuh luh) *noun*. cloud of gas

nectar (NEK tur) *noun*. a sweet liquid found in certain flowers

network (NET work) *noun*. a system of structures that cross one another

noble (NO bul) *adjective*. having greatness of character or worth

nocturnal (nok TUR nul) *adjective*. of or relating to the night

O

oceanographer (o shu NOG ruh fur) *noun*. a scientist who studies the oceans

opportunity (op ur TOO nuh tee) *noun*. chance

optical (OP tuh kul) *adjective*. having to do with sight

optical system (OP tuh kul SIS tum) *noun*. device that allows robots to "see"

orbit (OR bit) *noun*. the path of a satellite as it makes a complete revolution around a planet

outrageous (out RAY jess) *adjective.* grossly offensive to decency

oval (OH vul) *adjective.* resembling an egg in shape

P

padlocks (PAD lokz) *noun.* locks with bars that pass through a ring, then snap into the body of the lock

panels (PAN ulz) *noun.* flat pieces of material, such as wood, used as a surface for a painting

pioneer (pie uh NEER) *noun.* one who ventures into unknown territory

plaque (plak) *noun.* a flat piece of metal, wood, or stone that contains a message that honors a person or event

plaster casts (PLAS tur castz) *noun.* hardened shapes

platform (PLAT form) *noun.* a raised, flat structure used as flooring

pollen (POL un) *noun.* a fine dust of small spores that become the male cells of flowers

pollution (puh LOO shun) *noun.* the contamination of air, soil, or water by the discharge of harmful substances

precise (pruh SISE) *adjective.* very exact, without mistakes

preserve (preh ZURV) *verb.* to protect from harm or damage

prevented (preh VENT ed) *verb.* kept from happening

professional (pruh FESH uh nel) *adjective.* relating to work that requires specific training and study

public transportation (PUB lik trans pur TAY shun) *noun.* ways for many people to travel, such as buses and subways

pueblo (PWEB lo) *noun.* a permanent village or community of any of the Pueblo peoples, consisting of multilevel adobe or stone apartment dwellings

Q

quality (KWOL uh tee) *noun.* fineness, excellence

quarantine (KWOR un teen) *noun.* enforced isolation in order to prevent the spread of contagious disease

R

ramp (ramp) *noun.* a roadway, sloping up or down, sometimes connecting different levels

ransom (RAN sem) *noun.* the release of property or a person in return for payment of a demanded price

remodeling (ree MOD ling) *verb.* making over in structure or style

remote-controlled (ree MOTE kun TROLD) *adjective.* controlled from a distance by radioed instructions or coded signals

resented (ree ZENT ed) *verb.* felt indignant or angry

resist (ree ZIST) *verb.* to remain firm against actions or effects; withstand

ridges (RIJ ez) *noun.* raised strips

ridiculous (rih DIK yuh luss) *adjective.* absurd, silly

S

satellite (SAT ul ite) *noun.* an object launched to orbit Earth or another planet

scuba diving (SKOO buh DI ving) *noun.* swimming underwater with a special breathing device

sculptor (SKULP tur) *noun.* a person who shapes or carves a form in some kind of material, such as clay, stone, wax, snow, or ice

settlers (SET lurz) *noun.* people who move to live in a new place

shady (SHAY dee) *adjective.* of doubtful character; having a bad reputation

shocking (SHOK ing) *adjective.* highly disturbing emotionally

sightings (SI tingz) *noun.* viewings; times that you see something

simulator (SIM yuh lay tor) *noun.* equipment that generates test conditions that are close to actual conditions

slick (slik) *adjective.* clever and skillful

social (SO shul) *adjective.* part of a group

social worker (SO shul WUR kur) *noun.* a person who works to make things better for individuals and their community

soggy (SOG ee) *adjective.* filled with water; soaked

solo (SO lo) *noun.* a performance done by one person

sonar (SO nar) *noun.* a system that uses sound waves to locate objects

soothing (SOOTH ing) *adjective.* relaxing

space shuttle (SPASE SHUT ul) *noun.* a reusable spacecraft with wings for controlled descent into the atmosphere

spark (spark) *verb.* to move into action, stir up, excite

sphere (sfeer) *noun.* a celestial body, such as a planet or star

splattered (SPLAT urd) *verb.* splashed or spilled

sprint (sprint) *noun.* a fast race over a short distance

stalls (stalz) *noun.* booths or counters at which items are displayed for sale

stilts (stiltz) *noun.* posts or poles used as supports for a building

submersible (sub MUR suh bul) *noun.* something that can go underwater, such as a small vehicle

subtropical (sub TROP uh kul) *adjective.* of or relating to the area next to or near the tropics

succeeded (sek SEED ed) *verb.* accomplished something desired

suffered (SUF urd) *verb.* felt pain or distress

suspect (SUHSS pekt) *noun.* a person who is thought to be responsible for a crime

suspense (suh SPENS) *noun.* uncertainty about what will happen next

swayed (swayd) *verb.* swung from side to side

swift (swift) *adjective.* moving with great speed

technology (tek NOL uh jee) *noun.* the application of science to industrial or commercial purposes

terraces (TER uh sis) *noun.* steps for farming, in the side of a mountain

terra cotta (TER uh KOT uh) *noun.* a kind of clay used in pottery and building

thatch (thach) *noun.* a roof made of straw or leaves woven together

theft (theft) *noun.* the act of stealing

theories (THEE uh reez) *noun.* ideas or guesses about something based on some evidence

tomb (toom) *noun.* a place above or below ground for a dead body

tournaments (TOOR nuh mentz) *noun.* a series of games in which people or teams try to win a championship

toxic (TOK sik) *adjective.* poisonous

transpiration (tran spuh RAY shun) *noun.* loss of water to the air

trio (TREE o) *noun.* a group of three

tsunami (tsoo NAH mee) *noun.* a huge, powerful ocean wave caused by an underwater earthquake, landslide, or volcanic eruption

unbreakable (un BRAY kuh bul) *adjective.* not able to be figured out

under fire (un dur FIE ur) *adjective.* being attacked

unique (yoo NEEK) *adjective.* very unusual

universe (YOO nuh vurs) *noun.* all matter and energy, including the earth, the galaxies, and the contents of space, regarded as a whole

urban (UR ben) *adjective.* in or relating to a city

ushered (USH urd) *verb.* led or conducted

V

valve (valv) *noun.* a device used to control the flow of gases or liquids by blocking a passageway with a moving part

vapor (VAY pur) *noun.* the gas state of a substance that is solid or liquid at other temperatures

vehicles (VEE ih kulz) *noun.* devices or structures for transporting people or things

vents (ventz) *noun.* openings

victim (VIK tim) *noun.* one who is harmed or killed by another

video conference call (VID ee o KON fur ens kall) *noun.* a phone call displayed on a video monitor

W

weightless (WAIT liss) *adjective.* having little or no weight

weightlessness (WAIT liss ness) *noun.* the state of having little or no weight

wreck (rek) *noun.* a ruined ship, usually one that has sunk

Y

yakking (YAK ing) *noun.* talking (informal)

Z

zero gravity (ZEER o GRAV uh tee) *noun.* the condition of apparent weightlessness

Personal Word Bank

Words	Definitions

Personal Word Bank

Words	Definitions

Personal Word Bank

Words	Definitions

Personal Word Bank

Words	Definitions

Personal Word Bank

Words	Definitions